T0208291

MY JOURNEY:

A WORM'S EYE VIEW OF CANCER

MY JOURNEY:

A WORM'S EYE VIEW OF CANCER

MICHAEL BARKER

MY JOURNEY: A WORM'S EYE VIEW OF CANCER

iUniverse books may be ordered through booksellers or by contacting:

iUniverse
1663 Liberty Drive
Bloomington, IN 47403
www.iuniverse.com
1-800-Authors (1-800-288-4677)

Because of the dynamic nature of the Internet, any web addresses or links contained in this book may have changed since publication and may no longer be valid. The views expressed in this work are solely those of the author and do not necessarily reflect the views of the publisher, and the publisher hereby disclaims any responsibility for them.

Any people depicted in stock imagery provided by Thinkstock are models, and such images are being used for illustrative purposes only.
Certain stock imagery © Thinkstock.

ISBN: 978-1-4917-8913-1 (sc)
ISBN: 978-1-4917-8912-4 (e)

Library of Congress Control Number: 2016903629

Print information available on the last page.

iUniverse rev. date: 03/17/2016

CONTENTS

INTRODUCTION

Why bother to write another narrative on a much too tragically common disease? And it was a bother to put this all down on paper particularly when I'm still recovering from lymphoma cancer. My cancer experience is not the stuff of fine literature. The plot is simple – get well. The motive is clear – to survive. The goal here is to offer a single example of one person dealing with a totally unexpected life threatening disease. What was it like to suddenly discover you had such an illness? How did the treatment evolve? What would it have been good to know about doctors and hospitals before undergoing treatment? This narrative can be thought of as a conversation one might have with a cancer patient if not restrained by the fear of prying and insensitivity.

This is a worm's eye view. This is the view from the patient's limited elevation, very near the bottom, once the treatments start. This narrative exposes some of the peculiarities of the medical system that can only be revealed from the bottom up, from the humble patient. The narrative is not in any form a comprehensive review of the medical system or even of my own particular case. The reader is warned that the author has absolutely no medical background that would suggest any competency in criticizing the medical establishment. He only knows how the system feels to a single hurting cancer patient.

The doctors and nurses encountered in this journey were without exception outstanding individuals seemingly sometimes trapped in a system that confounds them as well as the patient. I am very grateful for their good work on my behalf, but not to the extent where I would not raise, hopefully in a positive way, some of their foibles and some of the faults of the "system."

Voltaire said "The art of medicine is in amusing a patient while nature affects the cure." This is simply not true today in the case of cancer. If it were not for modern research-based medical treatments I would have been condemned to an agonizing death in less than a year after diagnosis.

NORMAL LIFE

Living the good life, retired in beautiful Vermont, what's not to like? Sailing on Lake Champlain and playing tennis in the summer, skiing and snow-shoeing in the winter, and enjoying the fabulous changes in the seasons – I was enjoying the glories of mountain living at its best! Then when everything seemed so pleasant for a splendidly healthy 76 year-old, cancer strikes!

Why the surprise? While my mother died of cancer at the age of 46 all of her three sisters lived well into their 90's dying not of cancer but of old age. My mother's cancer of the uterus was explained by the exigencies of World War II. She worked in a defense plant with carcinogenic chemicals during the war. Any complaint about noxious chemicals would be considered malingering. Didn't we all know there was a war going on? As she was dipping her hands into chemicals and breathing asbestos polluted air her future second husband, my stepfather, was landing on Tarawa with the first wave of marines where the US would suffer 40% casualties. How could the exposure to a few chemicals not be suffered on the home front? Later her cancer was explained in family lore by these exposures to carbon tetra chloride and other toxic substances.

My father died at the age of 48 of a heart attack due to war injuries. There was little indication of cancer on my father's side of the family. Nevertheless, cancer is ubiquitous and probably lurks in every family. Now that I reflect on it my father's cousin, a welder of steel on skyscrapers in San Francisco died of stomach cancer. Lloyd Barker went back up to the high steel after a surgical inspection of his stomach in 1956 revealed that his cancer was inoperable. To say that he was tough was an understatement. He hunted and fished until this death in 1960. His wife, Kate Barker, lived to 104. She was honored for many years at the annual 1906 San Francisco earthquake celebrations as being the only living native San Franciscan survivor of that historic event. A factoid mentioned because they married at an early age and had the same life style with no apparent ill effects on Kate. Lloyd probably felt like me. Why cancer and me?

Retiring to Vermont for a person highly connected to California and particularly the San Francisco Bay Area is worth explaining to define normal life before cancer. I came to Vermont to practice architecture and city planning joining in partnership with an old friend and outstanding architect, Bob Burley. I met Bob when he was on the Board of Directors of the American Institute of Architects in 1970. At the time I was Director of Urban and Environmental Programs for the AIA (American Institute Of Architects) in Washington DC. By 1985 I was an AIA administrator, a member of "the college of cardinals" of AIA. Being in the same position for 12 years was causing me itchy feet. In 1985 both of my sons where away at university, my wife of 22 years had fallen love with another man, and I needed a change. Empty nesting it in DC for more of the same didn't appeal so I gladly accepted Bob's offer to join him in Vermont.

Bob was not your average small state architect. Before starting practice in Vermont he was associated with Saarinen's firm in Buffalo where he worked on Dulles Airport, the US Embassy in London, and the Gateway Arch in Saint Louis. Bob was credited with saving the arch when its two cantilever halves didn't meet. It was his idea to pack the inner skin with dry ice to shrink the structure so the final pin joining the two sections could be driven home. We had talked about getting together for 15 years. Suddenly it seemed time for me to join him in Vermont. We were fortunate to have many very interesting projects while we practiced together including the restoration of the Vermont State House and State Supreme Court, a two block project in Manhattan connected with the South Street Sea Port Redevelopment, two resorts for Laurence Rockefeller, and many ski resorts and commercial buildings.

I was sitting with Bob in our office, an old school house overlooking the Mad River, when Bob told me he had an offer to head up the Frank Lloyd Wright Foundation to restore Taliesin, Wrights famous iconic school of architecture in Wisconsin. Gazing out the window I asked him the size of the trees in the parking lot when he first started the office in 1965. He said there were no trees back then. I told him that he was watching trees grow and that was a bad sign. We agreed that he should take the Taliesin job while I continued to practice in Vermont. A few years later, I had an offer to become the Executive Director of The American Planning Association back in Washington, DC, where I kept a townhouse just in case I might return to Washington. I accepted.

After a few busy years back in Washington as the head of a national organization I began to miss the more leisurely pace of life in Vermont. I wanted the time to finish a book I was writing and planned to do more writing and truthfully more sailing and skiing as well so it was back to Vermont in 1996. Having had 18 years of enjoyable retirement when the cancer struck may earn little sympathy from those still laboring under the yoke of regular work with diminished expectations of a long happy retirement. At 76 what can one expect in additional years when the US average life span for a man is 76 years? When life is good time flies. The reality of the pointed top of the population pyramid seemed so far away, until it started to squeeze me with the onset of serious illness.

It is also my good fortune to have a large and interesting family. Two well careered and married sons (one a mechanical engineer and the other a motion picture executive), 26 cousins, many nieces and nephews and five siblings, all of them on the West Coast. We all enjoy each other immensely when we visit. My three granddaughters in Los Angeles are a special source of pride. My youngest son their father, brings them to Vermont regularly.

Indeed most of my family has come to visit me in Vermont over the years and of course I travel to Los Angeles, San Francisco, and Seattle to visit them.

So there I was living in my mountain top timber framed house with the great views of Lincoln Peak, Mount Abraham, and Sugarbush ski runs on 13 beautiful acres, minding my own business, doing the sports that I loved, and appreciating life sublime.

THE ONSET

The summer of 2014 started well enough. After a great deal of hard work, my sailboat (WINGDAM) was in great shape for the racing season on Lake Champlain. I bought the 1977 Tartan 34 C in 1980 while living in Washington DC. After five years of sailing on the Chesapeake Bay I sailed the boat up the East Coast to New York right past the Statue of Liberty and the glimmering World Trade Center building, then into the Hudson River. At the tidal headwaters of the Hudson at Troy New York, we entered the Champlain Canal successfully transiting its 12 locks to sail into Lake Champlain. The boat did very well racing on Lake Chaplain. Boating soon became a main summer activity. During the first two months of the 2014 summer WINGDAM won the Lake Champlain Yacht Club June and July Wednesday evening series races, her class in the July Mayor's Cup Regatta in Plattsburgh, NY, and several other weekend regattas. The summer of 2014 was off to a great start before the world turned upside down!

When not racing we also cruised the boat on non-race weekends to beautiful places on Lake Champlain. When I say "we" I mean Sigi and me. We have been together for almost 25 years in a loving relationship. While we do not live together full time, we do spend most of our weekends together. We also travel together, mostly to Europe and beyond, all immensely enjoyable! She does not race! For competition I have a fine crew of strong young men who relish challenging sailing. She likes fair weather, beautiful anchorages, and good company. She was the one who encouraged me to see my doctor when I complained that after sailing in the Mayors Cup I had blurry vision in my right eye and a slight numbness on my right upper lip.

She is quite aware of my optimism, hardheadedness, and reluctance to seek medical advice for trivial illnesses.

The compromised vision did bother me but it was manageable – I was still winning sailing races and playing tennis (poorly). On March 14th I had a complete wellness exam by my local doctor, Dr. Fran Cook, that showed me to be in perfect health. On March 28th I had a complete eye exam that also indicated healthy eyes. These were good signs that delayed me in seeking immediate treatment for the blurry vision in my right eye. I also had some numbing of my right lip that I attributed to a bite from some predatory Vermont insect. I spend a lot of time hiking in my woods, inadvertently coming into contact with deer ticks and black flies. Finally, on July 15th, at Sigi's urging I made an appointment to see a doctor at our local medical clinic, the Mad River Valley Health Center in Waitsfield. My doctor there, Dr. Cook, was on vacation. Dr. Katzman was filling in for Dr. Cook.

After an hour of examination Dr. Katzman suspected I had either a mild stroke or perhaps Lyme disease, carried by the deer tick. Blood tests quickly eliminated Lyme disease as the cause of my problems. The sonograms of my neck arteries were done in the Central Vermont Medical Center in Berlin, Vermont, about a 40- minute drive from my house. This is the closest hospital to my house. This hospital is affiliated with the University of Vermont Medical Center (CVMC) in Burlington, a much larger facility and the location of the medical school. Using this smaller hospital made sense because it is 20 miles closer to my residence than our state's main medical facility. The technician listening to the sonograms said my veins and arteries were clear like those of a 40 year-old man. That I didn't have a stroke, a constriction of the blood supply to the brain, was good news. However time was passing as my symptoms became more acute.

The next week I saw Dr. Chris Malcom at the Mad River Health Center who thought I might have a sinus infection. Never in my life did I have such an infection. She put me on antibiotics. The next weekend Sigi and I were visiting remote Stave Island on Lake Champlain with eight other Tartan 34 C sailboats. Over the weekend my symptoms became more acute. The next Tuesday my doctor, Fran Cook, was back in the office from his well-deserved vacation. He immediately sent me for a MRI of my head at the Central Vermont

Medical Center. On Thursday Dr. Cook called me to tell me I had a tumor in my sinus and behind my right eye. He set me up with an appointment on July 29th with Dr. Leopold, an Eye, Nose, & Throat specialist at The University of Vermont Medical Center in Burlington (UVMC), our big regional medical facility connected with The University of Vermont Medical School.

When I walked into Dr. Leopold's "office" I didn't know what to expect. He was a man in his mid 50's. His face was sympathetic and kindly, a good sign; or was he masquerading? The room had what looked like a dentist's chair in the middle. On a counter a computer screen displaying the MRI of my sectioned head glowed ominously. The doctor pointed out a grey mass in my sinus and behind my right eye in a tone that foretold of immediate pain to come if I had listened closely. Minimum introductory small talk was professionally brief. His full-length starched stiff white hospital coat suggested he was all business. His assistant Dr. Gorman, similarly attired, was a younger man ready for action. He was bouncing on the balls of his feet, appearing to be eager to get started. Once in the chair Dr. Leopold studied my tumor on the screen while Dr. Gorman prepared his examination instruments, long stainless steel rods with various devices on the ends. Soon I became aware that the rods were armed with a camera and cutting tools. Then it got ugly.

Dr. Gorman inserted the tools through my nose into my sinuses while Dr. Leopold watched the progress on a second computer screen offering directional guidance. The most difficult part happened when Dr. Leopold began asking for tissue samples of the tumor. My mind raced ahead imagining that one would be more than plenty. I was unable to speak, only croak. Ultimately five tissue samples were taken, enough to satisfy the lab folks who would be charged with finding out the cellular structure of my tumor. Dr. Leopold warned me that I would bleed down my throat for a while but not to worry. This was normal after a tissue sample was taken in the sinus. First blood I thought! When I stopped at a drinking fountain for a sip of water on the way out of the hospital the fountain tray turned bright red.

Dr. Leopold telephoned me the next morning informing me that I had aggressive B cell non-Hodgkin's lymphoma. His words had the hardness of steel and the heaviness of lead. It became clear to me that

I needed treatment quickly as my symptoms were rapidly getting worse. My right eye was closing and the numbness was spreading on my face. Dr. Leopold set up an emergency appointment with oncologist Dr. Julian Sprague for Friday, that unlucky first week of August. Dr. Sprague, a small trim man in his early 50's had a wry smile with a matching sense of humor. I spent an hour being examined by Dr. Sprague. His conclusions: 1) I was in great physical shape, 2) I needed treatment for my cancer as soon as possible, and 3) my amorphous tumor could not be surgically removed necessitating chemotherapy treatment.

We both agreed that because of the aggressive nature of my tumor that treatment should begin as soon as possible. Speedy Dr. Sprague arranged a bone and marrow exam, a heart evaluation, and copious blood work that very afternoon. The thought of a bone and marrow tests raised the question of how one gets the bone and marrow to test. I soon found out. Nurse Practitioner Paul Larson, about 40 years old, having the physique of a marathoner, and the sunny disposition of a evangelist, led us to a small operating room. He had me lay on my side with my left hip exposed. After some surgical preparation and local anesthesia he hammered a thin sharp hollow tube into my pelvis. During his prolonged efforts he complained about my hard bones. He observed that I must be a tennis player. The pain was tolerable. When he pulled the tube out he had his sample. The sample was then sent to the Pathology Department to see if there were cancer cells present. The bone and marrow exam showed no cancer cells

The heart exam used a sonogram of my heart in action. It was very interesting seeing one's organ pumping away. No problems there. Blood pressure was in the healthy range. There was no indication of a heart murmur I had as a kid, basically a leaky valve that seems to have fixed itself by running itself in. All indicators showed that my heart was sound enough to endure the ordeal of chemical-therapy. From diagnosis on July 29th to my first chemo injections on August 6th was just 8 days!

I was still trying to grasp that I had cancer. Moving back from that reality suggested it had to be some poor unfortunate soul, maybe an old friend or relative. No such luck. Life was beginning to revolve around this new, frightening reality. No more sail boat racing, social gatherings, tennis, strenuous physical activities, and alcohol (wine and beer). Medical procedures became daily life! Through all of the above Sigi was with me. Driving me three days a week to medical appointments in Burlington some 50 miles from my house. Suddenly I was losing control over my life, uncharacteristically depending on others, particularly Sigi, to get by each day. Not even having the luxury of crying in my beer dimmed all prospects.

On the morning of August 6th I had a surgical implantation of a PIC. This is an access in the arm to a major artery where the chemo chemicals can be inserted and mixed. It is also provides access to one's blood without putting more holes in the arm. This requires a tube deep into the circulatory system where blood will mix with the chemo chemicals drip by drip. On the afternoons of August 6th and August 7th I had a total of nine hours of chemical infusion into my PIC. Ten days later my right eye was returning back to its normal socket! It appeared that at least part of the tumor was shrinking from chemical attack. Those ten days did not go smoothly in any respect, but I was starting on the long road to recovery. To those around me it appeared that I chose to light a candle rather than curse the darkness. Actually I did both.

My final diagnosis concluded I had an aggressive extra nodal non- Hodgkin's B type lymphoma. The B cells regulate the immune system. Normally, the cells of the lymphoid system, lymphocytes, are arranged in clusters – called lymph nodes or lymph glands – or circulate though the bloodstream and the lymphatic channels to all the tissues of the body. Malignant lymphoma may occur in an isolated lymph node, a group of lymph nodes, in organs such as the stomach and intestine, the sinuses, bone, skin, or a combination of these sites. About 60,000 new cases are diagnosed each year in the U.S. Survival rate for five years after treatment averages 60%. Survival to 5 years is considered a cure. My case is somewhat special because the tumor was in my head making it dangerously close to my brain.

The eternal question is "why me?" when cruelly confronted by one's possible imminent mortality. Was this punishment by God for earthly transgressions? Could expected suffering be offered to reduce my time in purgatory? Would my prayers and those of family and friends be answered by a complete cure? Just what role did God play in this affliction? Should I surrender to the will of God if this is the will of God? Should I just accept the disease and rely on being in

God's hands? Or should I leave God out of this and get on with the treatments? Maybe we all carry a sleeping cancer tiger inside, and we can't predict when that bad cat will wake, stretch, and sharpen its claws.

Faith and spirituality are basic human instincts. The Roman Catholic faith played a historically strong role in my family. My great uncle, a Franciscan Priest, was the Prefect of the Franciscan order in the Western Hemisphere. My grandfather's three sisters joined Catholic teaching orders and served with distinction in missions in India and South America. One of my uncles, a clerical priest, became the Pastor of a large parish in San Francisco and produced and directed a religious Sunday morning television show, "Faith of Our Fathers." My mother raised our family in the Catholic tradition, from parochial schools to regular church going. I learned the Latin Mass serving my parish as an alter boy. What happened?

Today I am an unapologetic agnostic: unapologetic but not proud of it. Of my grandfather's 26 grandchildren, only six have kept up the traditional Catholic practice. Being part of a college educated-skeptical generation, I am without the total comfort of deep religious faith in my time of a life-threatening illness. During the Great Depression my religious grandfather reluctantly sent my mother to the University of California Berkeley; reluctantly because he thought that UC Berkeley was in the hands of atheists, communists and free love promoters. He lacked the funds to send her to a religious college. He actually fantasized that my mother of all people might follow family tradition and become a nun. She kept her faith, flourished at Cal and went into show business. Tempting fate and faith, I also went to UC Berkeley.

I have seen the serenity of cancer patients who have placed their lives totally in the hands of God. What great comfort! It's God's will they say. When my doctors told me they had no exact idea why I was picked out to join the other 60,000 new lymphoma cases in the U.S. each year, my inclination was to fault medical science, bad luck, or bad habits rather than God. That God would be interested in my paltry case, a case that dwarfs the torments being suffered among the worst off of the other 7.6 billion humans on the planet, strains credulity. Nevertheless glorious hypocrisy allowed me to accept all the prayers I was undeservedly blessed with! Just maybe!

Obviously getting one's spiritual life in order is important when getting hit on the head with one's mortality, in my case actually in my head. This of course also extends to getting one's more mundane "affairs" in order. For those with strong religious beliefs this can and should be a great help enduring cancer treatment. In spite of all the above my recommendation is to take a strong role in managing your treatment. Give God a hand! Extensive studies of deaths in hospitals suggest that over 440,000 deaths a year can be attributed to human error. Medical errors make patient harm in hospitals the nation's third leading cause of death, trailing heart disease and cancer. Doctors and hospital practices are not error free. Mistakes can include wrong diagnosis, medication mix-ups, and unsanitary transmittal of disease. The slogan "In God We Trust" should be tempered by Presidents Reagan's warning about the Soviets: "Trust but verify."

Letting go is not easy - letting go of "normal" life, letting go of life itself, although we all must go through this whatever the cause, and letting go of the future. In my case upon reflection I have concluded that my life on balance has been constructive. When asked on the edge of life what their life's contribution has been most people say it is their offspring. I would include my two fine sons in such a legacy. Also my professional career has given me the opportunities many do not have to engage in work that has benefited society. From engineering, to architecture to urban planning my professional work has gifted me with the notion that I have made a contribution to humankind during my brief existence. Whether or not this is self-delusional or is actually the case, what counts is that I believe it now and when I may be called on to let go.

Some would equate having cancer with a death notice. In desperate cases one might even consider ending it all to avoid the inevitable end-of-life suffering associated with the dreaded disease. It is truly like being a child lost in the wild imagined by Robert Service in his poem "The Quitter."

"When you're lost in the wild and you're scared as a child,
And Death looks you bang in the eye,
And you're sore as a boil it's according to Hoyle
To cock your revolver … and die.
But self-dissolution is barred.
In hunger and woe, oh it's easy to blow …
It's the hell-served-for-breakfast that's hard."

Mortality awareness for breakfast starts each day with cancer.

THE REACTIONS

Word was getting out that Michael Barker had cancer! Family, friends, assorted well wishers and the curious bombarded me with condolences and questions. My time doing emails each day went from one hour to five hours. Trying to sort out the frequency and detail needed to respond to each category of inquiry became a challenge. Of course family needed to know the details in real time. Close friends needed a little less detail. And the many others, former business associates, sailing and ski racing friends, neighbors, and acquaintances usually needed less detail. I began to realize that during my long professional life I had become a member of a number of communities through my work with the National Academy of Sciences, architectural practice, administrative positions, and world travel.

Initially, well wishers fell into two categories, those who wanted to console me and those who wanted to console me and to recommend the best cancer doctor for my condition. Suggestions for doctors came in from Los Angeles, Washington, DC, New York, and Boston. Several of my close friends even contacted world renowned cancer doctors of their acquaintance to possibly take on my case informing me to call them as they had already paved the way for my contact. Some suggested that being treated at a regional hospital in rural Vermont would not get me the best results. To get the best I would need to go to Los Angeles, New York or Boston. Grateful for the advice I was still in no mood to go outside of Vermont for treatment due to both convenience and potential quality of care.

The University of Vermont Medical Center (UVMC) Hospital is a very good teaching hospital connected with the University of Vermont Medical School and 50 miles from my house in Warren. In the end and to fend off these heartfelt suggestions, I wound up selecting Dana-Farber in Boston for my "second Medicare opinion." Dr. Farber is credited with virtually inventing chemotherapy. It turns out that my ski house neighbor on Fuller Hill helped raise $47 million for Dana-Farber, one of best cancer research hospital on the East Coast. He kindly arranged through the president of the hospital Board of Governors an "A" team to consult on my case. This helped curtail most of the general medical advice by non-medical folks. However, it did not slow down good wishes that included encouraging reports of complete cures of my exact type of cancer.

A frequently expressed sentiment coming by card and email was that Michael Barker was a tough and resilient person who could beat any cancer challenge. These nice thoughts were coming as my nose still hurt, my PIC spigots dangled from my right arm, my veins were holed, chemo shock was setting in, and I was summarily uprooted from a perfectly busy happy life. Honestly, I was only tough in a shaky Don Knots sort of way, simply because there was no alternative way to be. You really never know how tough you are until being tough is the only choice you have.

My A "team" at Dana-Farber was headed by Dr. Ann LaCasce. On Thursday, August 21st Sigi, both of my sons, and I drove down to Boston to meet with Dr. LaCasce. To see her we were required to visit a special office that tried to persuade me to enter into a clinical trial form of treatment. I resisted for two reasons. Firstly, to be in a clinical trial I would have to travel to Boston for some of the new treatments and evaluations. Secondly, according to "Big Jewels" (Dr. Sprague) my cancer was rather typical and not so far along that I needed to resort to "experimental" therapies, at least not right away. Dana-Farber was aggressively looking to line up more patients to experiment on while I was looking for a cure to my rather regular form of lymphoma. When we left the office of the very attractive sales nurse I could see she was disappointed.

Dr. LaCasce practices at Dana/Farber and teaches at the Harvard Medical School. At Harvard she is in charge of the post-doctoral students. Coincidentally, my oncologist at UVMC, Big Jewels Sprague, is also in charge of post-doctoral students going to The University of Vermont Medical School. Later I found out that Dr. LaCasce and Dr. Sprague knew each other quite well. The world of top oncology doctors is quite small on the East Coast. Dr. Sprague said he was in charge of 12 post-doctoral students while Dr. LaCasce was in charge of 30 post-doctoral students, alluding to the idea that he was her junior. To me this is not a negative. It means that Dr. Sprague might just have more time to work with his patients. The familiarity of my oncology doctors with each other did not compromise my view of the ability of Dr. LaCasce to be a reliable second opinion.

When all four of us entered Dr. LaCasce's examination room in downtown Boston we were greeted by her white smocked assistant in training, a fully qualified physician working under the master for clinical experience. She did a preliminary exam on me taking a lot of care in getting family background information, medical history, and vital signs. Earlier I had arranged to have all my medical tests and other records sent to Dr. LaCasce's office. A half hour later Dr. LaCasce swished in with a theatrical flourish. She is tall and stunningly beautiful woman of about 45. After introductions all round she had me hop up on the examination table. She examined me as my family looked on. She concluded that my treatment plan at UVMC was appropriate.

In conversational banter she revealed that she skied at Sugarbush, my local ski area. She said she rented a ski house with another family near the base area. She, her husband, and teenaged son planned to ski quite a bit during the season. I told her she could always rely on me to give her the "real" snow report if she was in question about the reports on the Sugarbush website before driving up from Boston implying I expected the same of her when discussing my illness.

Over the course of my treatment I found Dr. LaCasce to be responsive and very helpful. Whenever I called on her to review my case she got back to me on the phone either the same day or the next. She carefully reviewed the records and was always up to date. Having her as a second opinion was directly helpful and it was also beneficial to let the folks at UVMC know that I was getting a second opinion keeping them on their toes.

A curious aspect of being diagnosed with cancer is the reaction of both close and distant friends to the news. Having the dreaded cancer seems to alter your persona in the eyes of those who instinctively fear the disease. In the most drastic cases friends simply do not know how to relate to one who has been so afflicted. This leads to embarrassing pauses in conversation, clumsy language, and peculiar sentences that suggest speaking to someone already in the grave. This places the cancer patient in the position of reassuring the concerned friend that your specific cancer is not that serious when you are actually quite terrified of your prospects. Fortunately, I have found that a sense of humor can quickly dispel this strained atmosphere and provide the concerned friend space to adjust the new reality. Cancer like life is too serious to be taken seriously all the time.

A recent PBS series about cancer based on Dr. Siddhartha Mukherjee's book, "Cancer: The Emperor of All Maladies" asserts "more will die from cancer over the next two years than died in combat in all the wars the United States has ever fought, combined." If that isn't scary enough, Dr. Mukherjee a cancer doctor and author, observes in the same series "The very genes that make you grow, the very genes that keep you alive, will under different circumstances kill you." He also mentions that one out of two men and one out of every three women will have some form of cancer before they die. It is no wonder that even the mention of this scourge, this plague, puts terror into the hearts of all of us. When someone you know has cancer, something clicks in the brain, stimulating a sense of the horror of what is to come.

Medical research shows cancer is potentially in all of us. Those who look to an eternal God for an explanation of their affliction my find Shakespeare's Julius Caesar's advice on ill-fortune apropos. "The fault, dear Brutus, is not in our stars, but in ourselves."

As the word spread I began to receive cards from folks I had been out of contact with for 20 even 30 years, for example old neighborhood family friends who raised kids in Washington DC in the 70's and 80's. It's strange how intense shared experiences decades ago can leap time and geographical chasms. It was delightful and distracting to find out how their kids, now in their 40's and 50's were doing. Cancer, probably the threat of death, was the catalyst to reinvigorating these ancient relationships. Our culture hides certain mortality. When one of the old gang is on the brink folks tend to remember the good times. I was thankful to reestablish active contact with so many historic neighbors and associates.

Strong support from family and friends was crucial in the early months. Both of my sons generously came to help, one from Seattle and the other from Los Angeles. I joked that having cancer was a good way to get out of work, especially getting my mountain house ready for winter. Firewood needed moving and stacking, the boiler needed rebuilding, the roof ice deflectors needed to be refastened, and drainage ditches needed cleaning not to mention general mowing and upkeep. The chemo poisons weakened me too much to undertake these normal seasonal country living chores myself. My sons were quite aware of our family tradition of "do everything yourself."

Fueling all this work was Sigi who turned out three hearty meals every day. Sigi's expertise in the kitchen was matched by my hard-working talented sons' capabilities in roofing and plumbing. I'll never forget my youngest son hanging onto an extension ladder, strong legs trembling, anchoring 50 pounds of angle iron on a slick standing seam roof! Nor will I ever forget my older son tearing down and rebuilding my big propane gas boiler including all the electrical components. A movie executive on the roof and an engineer under a boiler, that's dedication and pure acts of love!

In a fortunate serendipity I had, as they say, gotten my business affairs in order. In the spring of 2014 long before there was any indication of cancer I thought it was time to get my will updated, a trust formed, medical directives completed, and my finances simplified. It took four months to complete this work working with a lawyer who specialized in estate planning in Waterbury, VT. Chris, my eldest son was enlisted to be my legal guardian should I be incapacitated. He also agreed to be the Executor of my estate. While he lives in the Seattle area he generously spent three weeks at my Warren house when I started cancer treatments. During this period we met with my attorney, who would be his attorney if worst came to worst. This relieved me of much stress. I let Dr. Big Jewels Sprague know that I was ready to pass on because my affairs were in order with the admonition that I was in no hurry to test my preparations. Because life is so unpredictable my advice to all adults is to get your affairs in order particularly an advanced directive on health care.

LIFE IN CHEMOTHERAPY

The "standard of care" for lymphoma treatment is chemotherapy. The tumors are not usually removable with surgery since they are amorphous masses. In my case the tumor in my sinus was detectable in the MRI of my head as a shaded area about 3x5 inches in my right sinus extending up behind my right eye. The complexity of the head bones and the involvement of my tumor with the bone structure made chemotherapy the best and only way to go. The treatment for me called "Rchop" was pretty standard mixture of chemotherapy that had been used clinically for about two decades.

Each year the taxpayers fund the National Institute of Health to the tune of $4.9 billion to research the cure for cancer. Over $40 billion is spent each year by the private sector on cancer research and development. Internationally about $20 billion is spent each year seeking cures for cancer. Yet all this investment has not produced any major breakthroughs for the treatment of non- Hodgkin's lymphoma. I was hoping for a kinder treatment more targeted to the cancer cells themselves rather than the blunderbuss approach of historic chemotherapy affecting all cells including healthy cells with its many side effects.

There are several new approaches in clinical trials that in the future will be much less destructive to the patient. They work with the patient's own immune system and in some cases with stem cells. In another ten years these treatments may be the new "Standard of Care." If my impatient lymphoma could have been more patient waiting to emerge until my late 80's, I might have been spared "Rchop" chemicals rituximab, cyclophosphamide, doxorubicin, vincristine, and prednisone. After considering clinical trails vs. the current "Standard of Care" approach, perhaps naively I chose the latter, deciding on a conservative approach most likely to succeed.

This narrative is not intended to be a clinical recitation of the treatments I received. On the contrary, I hope to convey what it felt like being treated for cancer from the worm's eye view. Until my personal encounter with cancer I was only vaguely acquainted with chemotherapy gained through TV, watching suffering people reclining in dismal rooms attached to bags of chemicals before they died. Was this to be my lot for the next four months? In addition, after the chemo, 17 radiation sessions were prescribed (ending on January 21, 2015). In sum, my full treatment took about six months. To get back to normal health an optimistic schedule would add another 4-6 months, notwithstanding any complications.

My first chemo session was scheduled for August 6th, just nine days after diagnosis. As mentioned earlier my case was treated as an emergency since my symptoms were becoming more acute by the day. I am very grateful for the swift actions of the doctors and nurses to get my treatment going. This required changing some of the normal procedures for treating cancer. For example, usually a PET scan (positron emission tomography) of the patient's whole body would be done before any treatment to determine the location and extent of the cancer. In my case this was not done until I already had two chemo infusions. The PET scan injects the patient with a radioactive isotope that can find cancer cells. Combined with a CAT X-ray scan a 3 dimensional color image of the body shows where the cancer is. On August 12th the PET scan of my whole body showed cancer only in my sinus area. The PET scan is 82% effective, effective meaning 18% of cancers remained undetected.

So how to get the chemicals into the bloodstream? At 8:00 am on the morning of my first chemo session I had a PIC installed in my right arm. In this procedure a tube is inserted into an artery with access toggles sticking out of the patients arm. Once the tube is in place an ex-ray is taken to make sure the tube is positioned in the chest properly. The dangling spigots were kept in place by elastic netting. Two weeks later the fragile PIC would be removed and a permanent port would be surgically installed under the skin on my right chest, same idea with a tube going to the jugular vein. As my treatment progressed I was very glad to have a port that made taking blood samples, adding enhancers to MRIs and CAT scans, and chemo injections relatively painless. Also the fewer new holes in my body the better.

Chris, my older son visiting from Seattle, drove me to the hospital for the surgical installation of the port. While I laid on the gurney in my funny hospital gown a guy walks over to me and says: "I heard you were in here Mike. How are you?" I finally recognized him as a fellow sailor and member of Lake Champlain Yacht Club who keeps his boat near mine in Shelburne Shipyard. Chris Morris and I had helped each other out over the years during preparations for spring launch. He is also an avid racer. I asked him what he was doing here. I knew he was a doctor of some sort never having imagined I would see him standing over me as his patient. Men sanding the bottoms of boats covered from head to toe with toxic bottom paint can easily make one forget about real life jobs. Boatyards are great equalizers. He said he ran this surgical department for the hospital. I told him I had to haul my boat due to being ill so my racing days this year would be over - except that our mutual sail maker, aware of my illness, asked me to crew on his boat whenever I wanted to race. Dr. Morris said I would be crazy to race until this cancer was beaten. I took his advice. Nevertheless I optimistically ordered and paid for a new racing genoa for the 2015 season.

On August 6th and 7th the chemo began. The hospital had four bays with four reclining chairs each. Each bay was run by special nurses who sat in the center of the space at a computer desk. All the nurses were young women, most of them very pretty. The space was cheery. Most of the chairs had views of a roof garden. In good weather one could tow their injection machine out to the roof garden to catch some sun. It was the upbeat and positive nurses who made those being treated feel as comfortable as possible.

The patients ranged from strong and healthy like me, at least in the beginning, to some who were attached to life by a thread. Patient ages ranged greatly, from a semi-comatose frail 90-year-old-man with metastasized lung cancer on chemo maintenance to a young beefy football player with testicular cancer, who reminded me that Lance Armstrong won five Tour de France's with only one ball. He joked he was on "Rejuvenuts" therapy. One afternoon I met an attractive woman, thin and about 50 years old, who said she had been fighting cancer for nine years. She sadly confided that she was on a new batch of chemicals as a last resort before Hospice care. With cancer you can always find someone who is worse off than you are.

The chairs were spaced such that conversation between chairs was difficult. Some very sick patients wanted and needed privacy. Others wanted to talk. Each chair had its own movable computerized monitor. The monitor held the chemo bags and the computer controlled injection machine. It was possible to get out of the chair and walk to the bathroom or visit around the ward towing your monitor behind you thus never missing a drop. When a bag was near empty a sound signal alerted the nurse that you were ready for another bag. In my case I went through 4-5 bags each session.

At both ends of the ward there was a galley stocked with sandwiches, soft drinks, and home-baked chocolate chip cookies. Volunteers often brought in special-baked treats to add to the ward's official fare. Sigi usually made our sandwiches and brought our drinks. However, when I became aware that a fresh batch of cookies or other goodies arrived I would tumble out of my chair, grab my monitor, and hustle to the galley for my share. I had cancer after all. Self-indulgence is therapeutic. If worse came to worse I didn't want to feel like one of those fat men on the "Titanic" that fateful night who said "No thank-you" to desert!

The chairs each had a suspended TV and audio setup. I didn't use these distractions. Once I got settled into my chair the nurse covered me with a thin preheated blanket, hooked me up to the drip bags on the monitor, and made sure I was comfortable. The initial drips included relaxing medications and saline solutions for hydration. The hospital had a special pharmacy for chemotherapy. Curly the pharmacist, named for his impressive mop of curly black hair, brought the bags of chemicals to each patient's chair-side locker. At this point the patient's identification was re-checked by Curly and the nurse. It seems that the hospital orders the chemo chemicals in huge drums. I had visions of rail cars on a siding being offloaded by diesel forklifts. Even for my standard "Rchop" the chemicals were specially mixed just before the infusions. When I questioned a nurse about putting all refuse in a hazardous waste bin she said that virtually all the chemo chemicals were very caustic. She said one drop could burn a hole in the skin! Very reassuring!

The cancer ward would be my life for six 21-day cycles of chemotherapy. Every designated Wednesday at 10:00 am I would show up to have my blood taken and my weight and blood pressure checked. After the 4-6 hour of infusions I received a special "horse shot" in the back of my arm. The shot's purpose was to protect at least a few white cells in my body. Toward the end of my chemotherapy I met a senior nurse who was able to give me this injection without the agony. I asked what her trick was. She said most nurses don't wash off all the disinfectant before shoving in the needle. She said the worst pain was caused by the disinfectant penetrating the skin and muscle.

When I emerged from my first chemo infusion and walked somewhat dazed into the waiting room area I was unexpectedly met by a smiling Thea Platt. After a big hug Thea handed me a CARE package of cancer necessities including laxatives, facemasks, a blood pressure monitor, a pill dispenser and organizer, and lots of chocolate bars. Bob her husband had survived serious lymphoma. He was "cured" just a year earlier. They both are members of The Lake Champlain Yacht Club where we were casually acquainted. Fellow cancer travelers seem to be in a special club unto themselves. It would be a gross understatement to say that this gesture of support was generous. It was loving and kindly in the extreme. There were other folks from my sailing club and neighborhood who had cancer strike close to them who also unexpectedly showed me unusual concern and kindnesses during chemotherapy. This was in stark contrast to all the hate and self-inflicted misery inundating TV. Real personal loving acts of gigantic kindness do happen. Thank-you Platts and all the others who helped me through tough times!

While my chemotherapy was set for four months the doctors were talking about additional spinal infusions of chemo to protect my brain from errant cancerous lymphoma cells that could possibly escape the regular chemo. Having cancer in the head apparently caught the attention of the cancer team at the hospital where all the cancer doctors at UVMC discuss cases once a week. Head cancers are dangerously close to the brain. Subsequently "Big Jewels" and Anne LaCasce discussed my tumor and decided it would be a good idea to infuse my spinal fluid with chemo that would get to my brain past the brain/body blood barrier. Just the sound of a spinal tap sounded awful and painful. However, since all the doctors agreed that this should be done I acquiesced. My new schedule would now include a spinal infusion on every Friday of the week of regular chemo. One puts up with these things by a sheer act of numbing acceptance.

Nurse Practitioner Paul Larson did the spinal work that involved removing a vile of spinal fluid and replacing it with the same exact volume of chemo. He was a trim marathon runner in his 40's. The site of the penetration at the base of my spine was treated with lidocaine, very much like a dentist's novacaine. Paul did hundreds of these procedures each year. He was good if that adjective can be used to describe the painful inevitable. Only one time did he hit something with his needle that caused me to reflexively jump up from my bent over posture knocking over his work table and sending his surgical drape flying.

One time when I was waiting in the treatment room for Paul, actually for "Curly" who was late in mixing the chemo, I thought I'd read the instructions on the surgical kit Paul used. The instructions were printed on the lid of the plastic 12x20 inch tray. One section said: "don't bend or break the needle!" When Paul came in I mentioned that if he bent or broke the needle in me the hospital would probably take it out of his pay. He explained to me nicely that patients were not supposed to read doctor stuff, particularly before a delicate procedure.

So what were the effects on me from chemo aside from some early and welcomed relief of my right eye distress? It was all the usual things you hear about cancer treatment. By the second month I was totally bald and hairless, including no beard, no eyebrows, and no pubic hair. My son Chris gave me a visor that had big hair tumbling out of the top for laughs. However I found the fake hair actually helped keep my baldhead warm. Most of the women undergoing chemo wore wigs. The nurses liked my headgear.

One symptom that plagues many chemo patients is nausea. Thankfully, I was generally spared this torment although I felt a bit green from time to time. At each chemo session I was infused with anti-nausea drugs that were designed to last three days. During the whole chemo treatment I did not take the supplemental anti-nausea pills I was prescribed; indicating either that my symptoms were mild or revealing a basic anti-pill disposition. Both are true. Also Sigi's made a special effort to make food that was attractive and easily digestible. If on the rare occasion my stomach felt queasy I postponed eating. Over the course of four months of treatment I lost about ten pounds of weight due to the debilitating effect of the chemicals. My weight loss was not due to nausea-induced lack of caloric intake; remember all the chocolate chip cookies?

Another pesky side effect of chemo is not being able to sleep. F. Scott Fitzgerald said "the worst thing in the world is to try to sleep and not to." I have never been afflicted by insomnia. This was something totally new to me. In chemo insomnia seems due to general discomfort of the chemical imbalances in the body. You don't hurt terribly in any specific place; you just feel generally ill, a consuming malaise of varying intensities. During the day one is distracted by the body's sensory inputs and just getting along with life. At night when all's quiet, lurking insecurities and pain sneak into a dark bedroom. For real pain I was prescribed Oxycodone, the stuff kids around here steal from pharmacies for highs. I never felt in enough pain to take this strong medication. Otherwise the prescribed medicine is ordinary enough, Tylenol PM. It worked sometimes – two tablets before bedtime and another tablet every 3 hours. Some nights were just bad nights with no sleep when the body just would not give in to peaceful sleep. The sleepless night knows all my secrets.

Another side effect of chemo that I should have been warned about more vigorously by the medical staff was constipation. I knew from TV ads that constipation was a national problem like the national debt; but unlike the national debt it was not mine. Regularity was simply not on my mind when I started with chemo.

After my first infusions suddenly my bowel movements, or lack thereof, became first a curiosity, then a worry, and then an emergency. On the Saturday at the end of my very first week of chemo Sigi and I rushed to the emergency room of the UVMC hospital. I had become so constipated there was only blood coming from my rectum. The emergency room doctor, Dr. Hudson, working with a nurse was able to get things moving after two hours of the most misery I've ever had. It surely was some misery for them with the unpleasant chipping, tugging and irrigating. Not ever having had bowel or colon problems in my life I learned very quickly this is no laughing matter!

We did have a good laugh however during this grotesque time when the nurse asked naked me to turn over exposing my privates to Sigi who was sitting in a chair 3 feet away. She suddenly asked if we knew each other. We reassured her that we were OK with this southern exposure. She said she had a man patient perform the same maneuver the previous week and it turned out the woman in the view seat was just a kindly and now shocked neighbor who brought the man to emergency.

After this lesson I spent the rest of my chemotherapy religiously taking ample laxatives and stool softeners. It took several weeks to get regular if there is such a thing as a regular gastro/intestinal tract when doing chemo.

During the six 21-day cycles of chemo, one becomes progressively weaker. Within each cycle there is also a progression. During the first ten days after chemo the body weakens till it reaches the depth of the valley of fatigue. One bad morning just getting dressed was nearly impossible due to fatigue. Then it starts to gain equilibrium – a good sign that there is hope. Then during the final week before the chemo starts again one can sense the body regaining some of its strength.

One feels like HAL the computer in the movie "Space Odyssey" as the crew of the space ship pulls out computer chip after computer chip trying to stop the misbehaving machine. HAL sings "Mary Had a Little Lamb" slower and slower like an old spring winding down until nothing. The cyclical downside is that inevitably the body winds down becoming weaker in each cycle. It would be euphemistic to say I was merely happy to complete the chemo phase of my cancer treatment.

This is not to suggest that all forms of chemo have the same effects on all patients as mine did. I spoke with some folks who experienced few problems with chemo. At a big Thanksgiving dinner at a neighbor's house I spoke with an old friend who had colon cancer. He had a full regimen of chemotherapy without even losing his hair! In January he had a section of his large intestine removed. The surgery was successful. He is now back in the saddle again as the chair of our municipal Development Review Board. A woman I spoke with who was on her second bout of breast cancer chemo told me it was easier the second time around. For me I hope to never revisit chemo again in any form.

On my last day in the chemo chair all the nurses gathered in our bay near my chair for the traditional celebration of chemical graduation. This ceremony was a total surprise. I stood at the center of the chemo bay like the fake celebrity that I was. I was handed a big school bell to ring and was invited to make a few remarks. There were 12 beautiful nurses standing there ready to hang on my every word, or so I fantasized. I thanked them for all their hard work on my behalf and made it plain that they would no longer be able to "have their way with me." I rang the bell and after sweet handshakes and a few hugs they ambled off back to their duties. Some in the bay seemed to be cheered up by one of their own being released. However, the thought struck me that all those folks still taking chemo on a maintenance program might only be reminded of their chemical shackles.

Along the way I had two more enhanced MRI's of my head and two enhanced CAT scans of my whole body. I also had a final PET scan on October 27th that showed no cancer. The radiologist's reports on these scans found other things wrong with me that I was totally ignorant of, like a belly button hernia. Pressing "Big Jewels" on these reports he said I was in perfect health for a man of my age. Actually, one radiologist specifically found that my brain was normal for a man my age. He obviously did not consult Sigi. I can't imagine how I would have felt if I received a typical humorless radiologist report carefully looking for cancer, only to find Alzheimer's or a brain tumor.

I believe that it is not a blessing to know everything that is wrong with you, particularly if there is nothing to be done. I could have passed on knowing about my slightly clogged arteries, my hidden hernias, and my other signs of an extended life well lived. My skeleton, my tissues, and my blood are now matters of public record. I do not feel it is an invasion of my privacy to be so exposed. On the contrary perhaps I'm the only one who is disadvantaged by knowing too much.

On the other hand I did request all the full reports on all tests I received. Most of this material never reaches the patient. In some cases it requires the specific request of the physician to release test results to patients, for good reason. The unsophisticated patient may needlessly worry about technical test results best left to a doctor to interpret. My case exactly; however, having a technical bent I wanted everything to make up my own ignorant mind. On balance I'm glad I did receive all the test results. Heck I paid for them! "Big Jewels" and his henchmen did assuage my fears by assuring me that for a specimen of my age I was in very good shape.

One of my many shortcomings is I forget how old I really am! At my age (77) I remember my grandfather spending his latter days sitting in a big comfortable chair in the sunroom of their San Francisco house in the shadow of Twin Peaks reading religious texts and meditating; this in stark contrast to my skiing and playing tennis. When my grandfather was younger and an active consummate booster of the glories of San Francisco he commissioned a monumental statue of Saint Francis by famed sculptor Bennie Bufanno that was placed on one of the twin peaks now visible from his chair. Who's to say which lifestyle is preferable?

The above description of my chemo treatments is abbreviated in that many other things were going on during this four-month six-cycle process. There were scans, blood tests, and doctor appointments to arrange which brought out the flaws in the "medical system."

Getting the results of tests at the beginning was problematic to say the least. Scans would be done, blood would be taken, and procedures undertaken with virtually no report to me on the results. I mentioned this to my younger son, Matt a motion picture executive, who watched in dismay his mother's tragic death in Arizona from ovarian cancer eight years earlier. She was tormented in her last four months of life by needless operations and lack of pain management. Her husband seemed to be of little help. Matt went directly to the hospital administration to straighten the situation out even having a personal discussion with the hospital CEO. This experience made him sensitive to my situation concerning test results. He asked me if I would object to his intervention on my behalf at UVMC. Visions of nurses giving me extra deep injections due to being a troublemaker crossed my mind. I told him to go ahead and try anyway.

Two days after Matt dealt with UVMC administrative leadership the test results started to appear on my "MyHealthOnline" account. Indeed Dr. Sprague telephoned me at home that evening to review several test results. I asked Matt how he got such fast results. He modestly said everybody works for somebody. He deals with the heads of movie studios and producers every day and one gets to know where the decision-makers are and how to stimulate them. It was like he turned over a big flat rock at UVMC and precipitated a lot of scurrying around. In the course of his work Matt discovered the hospital had an Office of Patient Advocacy. He put me in touch with the head of that department who remarkably had a daughter who was in Hollywood trying to make it in motion pictures. After Matt's intervention I made use of this office several times described below. It is important for all patients to know that virtually all hospitals have departments of patient advocacy.

On one occasion I was trying to confirm the time and place of a CAT scan. I telephoned the oncology department at UVMC. After holding long distance for about 35 minutes while repeatedly listening to a hospital recording extolling the virtues of "MyHealth Online" accounts where all medical results are posted, where all appointments are listed, and where all procedures can be found right up to date for each patient. This of course isn't true. Finally a guy named Mike came on the line from the hospital Communications Department advising me apologetically that there was nobody in the whole Oncology Department that could help me. I knew there were about 20-30 people working there at the time.

My recourse was to call Patient Advocacy for help. That evening a nurse from Radiation called me providing me with the time and place for the CAT scan. Early the next morning I received two calls from nurses, one from Oncology and another one from Oncology/Radiation advising me of the time and place of the scan. Unfortunately only one of the calls was correct – the one emanating from the Radiation Department where the scan would actually take place. Another call to Patient Advocacy helped sort this out. Otherwise I would have been calling the hospital once again, holding long distance, and thinking unpleasant thoughts about hospital communications.

Another situation arose when I wanted to make sure the results of tests were getting to where they should actually go, including to my general doctor, Dr. Fran Cook and Dr. Anne LaCasce at Dana-Farber. When I found out this was not happening it was necessary to visit with the communications group in each department after a test or procedure to make sure they delivered properly.

In the case of Dana-Farber I actually requested and received a disc of a PET scan that I physically carried to Boston lest the inter-hospital email failed. Once again I resorted to the Patient Advocacy Department to help stimulate the UVMC to do what should be automatic. Soon the links worked better even to the extent that test results where appearing on "MyHealthOnline." General advice to patients is that you are your best advocate.

Also take notes! Both Sigi and I made notes in meetings and telephone conversations with caregivers. Notes covered scheduling, prescriptions, and general treatment questions. Always date your notes and file them for quick reference. When appointments are scheduled with doctors come prepared with your questions and observations. A Doctor's time is precious as is yours when with your doctor.

One area that was problematic in my treatment was scheduling tests and procedures that would minimize my long commute to the hospital. The doctors seemed to want to wait till the last moment when I wanted a long-range treatment schedule. Several times I had to commute two days in a row when had these services been scheduled earlier one trip would have sufficed. The "system" is not automatically sensitive to the patient's needs in this respect. In scheduling the hospital comes first unless the patient lets the doctors and nurse schedulers clearly and forcefully know about your specific preferences.

In spite of my "troublemaking" ways I did not ever experience any retribution from doctors or nurses; Quite the opposite. When I mentioned inter-departmental barriers to communications for example, they recognized the problem sympathetically. Unfortunately, other than complain about the problems they were not in a position to do much about them. These highly skilled medical practitioners were far too busy treating patients. With all the complicated computer systems and modern management techniques developed in the last 50 years one is reminded of Orson Welles's famous ad lib in "The Third Man," that the Borgias' reign of bloodshed gave rise to the Renaissance while two centuries of democracy in Switzerland produced the cuckoo clock. In many respects hospital administration still cuckoos.

LIFE IN RADIATION

Having been ragged out from chemo I had no desire to begin radiation treatment. However the doctors ganged up on me. My treatment would be in another department. I would be going from Oncology to Oncology/Radiation. The key research showed that with cancers like mine where there was some bone involvement radiation gave the patient a 3-7 % better chance of total remission. The idea is that some cancerous lymphoma cells could still be lurking in bone tissue where regular chemo couldn't reach. So I met the Mel Gibson of radiology, Dr. Jim Wallace, a direct descendent of William Wallace of "Braveheart." Dr. Wallace actually plays the pipes in international competitions. Here I was about to embark on another cancer treatment with known bad side effects with slight benefits.

Sigi and I met with Dr. Wallace, who is also the head of the Oncology/Radiation Department, on December 5th, 2014. He is a man of about 50 years with a stout Scotsman-like build, no kilt but easy to imagine him swaying in step with other bag pipers. He had recently traveled to Glasgow Scotland with 40 other pipe players from Vermont for an international competition where the Vermonters placed 14 out of 60 teams. The density of pipers in Vermont seemed extraordinary. Dr. Wallace was modest about his great accomplishments in music. About medicine he was equally modest about what he had to offer me.

When I first started cancer treatment both "Big Jewels" and Anne LaCasce seemed to be reluctant to include radiation in my treatment program. They both were aware of a German study of malignant head tumors like mine whose outcomes were not improved with radiation. While waiting between appointments at UVMC I found a medical research library open to the public with a very pretty research librarian with time on her hands. She helped me find the German studies and even made copies for me. A careful reading of the studies revealed they did indeed show that there was some improvement in survival using radiation if the lymphoma had bone involvement. When there was no bone involvement then radiation did not improve survival rates and only caused problems of is own with nasty side effects.

Unfortunately, in my case the orbit bone under my right eye did show erosion due to the lymphoma. My three MRIs clearly showed this. That's how I was directed to consult with Dr. Wallace. Both "Big Jewels" and Anne LaCasce now thought that radiation was worth considering. Dr. Wallace said he could only offer me 3-7% better chance of survival (five years) with radiation. He said there was the possibility that my cancer might be totally cured already. He was well aware of the German studies. He also discussed the side effects of radiation including: permanent damage to the saliva glands, increased possibility of cataracts in the eyes, potential skin cancers, unspecified dental deterioration, local hair extinction, and general fatigue. Sigi and I looked at each other. What to do? The question was how lucky did I feel?

Once I was diagnosed I took to the Internet to study what lymphoma was all about. Checking survival rates was not encouraging. It appeared that the average patient with lymphoma had about a 50/50 chance of surviving five years after diagnosis. Some groups of patients with specific types of the disease had up to 90% survival. Much depended on how quickly the cancer was found, the age of the patient, the physical condition of the patient, the location of the tumor and whether the lymphoma cells had "markers" that made treatment more difficult. On the bad side I am old at 77 and the cancer was in my head. On the good side I was in exceptional physical condition, the illness was discovered early, and the pathology showed no "markers." This placed me in the 75% survival group in my optimistic guestimate.

Neither "Big Jewels" nor Dr. Wallace would be pinned down on my exact chances of survival out to five years. Friends who had friends who beat lymphoma reminded me more than once that I was tough enough to do likewise – encouraging but not definitive. I hoped to live about another ten years. If the next ten years went as fast as the previous ten years this seems a modest goal. Living is traveling, playing tennis, writing, painting watercolors, sailing my boat, skiing, eating well and getting around, all requiring reasonably good health. Cancer is full of probabilities, is definitely not an exact science, and is baffling when imaging a future.

What finally persuaded me go ahead with radiation was psychological not pathological. To be haunted by the possibility of the lymphoma returning when with some radiation I could have been clean cinched the deal. I would never forgive myself if I turned down the radiation that just might have been able to effect a cure. Yes, it increased my chances by only 3-7%. To me it was well worth the gamble to avoid another round of chemo. Second time around chemo for lymphoma is less effective than the first round and certainly more debilitating. Also in my investigations I found reference to lymphoma cells being more vulnerable to destruction by radiation than other cancer cells opening up the prospect that the actual doses might be less in my case incurring less severe side effects. With cancer there are no perfect choices, only choices that are both bad and less bad.

Dr. Wallace said I would need 17 radiation treatments every weekday starting on December 29th and ending on January 20th. The first step would be making a facemask for me that would precisely locate the radiation beams into my head at exact points. Two skilled nurse practitioners heated up a plastic membrane and forced it over my face. Soon it became rock solid. Then a mold of the back of my head, phrenology bumps included, was made using a fast setting plaster. These two parts then were joined by a clamping system that attached my head to a sliding bed. Once locked in I was unable to move. Each of the 17 treatments required being re-clamped into the mask. The nurses were not amused when I referred to my mask as a death mask even after I told them the story about the death masks of Michelangelo and Leonardo di Vinci located in Santa Croce Church in Florence. I should have known by the look of her that the very pregnant Viet Namese radiologist nurse was not keen on feeble radiation levity.

The immense radiation machine was implanted in a wall of the lead-lined treatment room. Much of the mechanism was located in a mechanical room behind the wall. Visible to the patient is a moving "bed," and a huge revolving donut with movable spigots and lenses. Once locked in all the nurses eagerly flee to the safety of a radiation proof control room before the radiation beams are shot into the patient's body. The painless radiation took only ten minutes to complete. While being zapped I could see bright red lights go on and off through my eyelids and the semitransparent plastic mask. As the machinery worked it sounded like I was inside of a poorly loaded dishwasher.

Each patient's special radiation treatment is preprogramed into the computer that drives the huge contraption. As I was being immobilized flat on my back underneath the intimidating machine I did wonder if the 2-3 technical nurses, never the same group each session, correctly programed the mega-machine for my specific needs. I was only slightly reassured by my name being prominently scrawled on my mask that this was all for me.

My confidence was somewhat sustained by the fact that all the radiation equipment was relatively new. Four years ago the hospital had three new ELEKTA machines installed in three new treatment rooms. Made in Sweden the machines are sold all over the world. If one invested $17 in an EKEKTA (OMX) share five years ago, today it would be worth over $50. Being treated by state-of-the-art machinery made by a highly rated company provided some comfort. I was granted a peek at the back of the machine after three sessions. It looked like a two-ton space ship stuck to a heavily reinforced wall. All the mechanisms that moved the radiation beams were controlled by computer driven servos and motors behind the "curtain" reminding one of the great Wizard of Oz only without human intervention.

Dr. Wallace told me that each machine cost $7 million alluding to the real reason for the high cost of medicine. Obviously runaway medical costs could not be blamed on high physician's pay. For one of my MRI head scans the hospital charged $5,000. There is an enterprising businessman here in Vermont who wants to do similar MRIs for $750. So far he has spent $40,000 trying to get a required "Certificate of Need" permit from the state. It will be interesting to see if the state is more interested in protecting vested hospital interests or in adding a modicum of competition to lower medical testing costs. Without getting bogged down in this complicated subject all that can be said here is that hospital billing costs do seem to be outrageously high.

While somewhat out of chronological sequence in this narrative major test results taken near the end of chemotherapy and during early radiation were coming in with generally positive results. On October 27th, 2014 I had the final results of a NM PET CT EYE TO THIGH. As mentioned earlier, the PET scan uses radioactive isotopes to identify the presence of cancer cells. To quote radiologist Dr. Kikut's report: "Resolution of residual uptake this patient's right sinonasal mass. No additional sites of abnormal radiotracer uptake to indicate residual lymphoma." Additional finding included: "There are atherosclerotic calcifications of the coronary arteries and aorta. Degenerative changes are seen throughout the spine. Sclerotic lesions within the left proximal femur are unchanged likely representing small bone islands. A tiny nodule within the superior segment of the left lower lobe is stable. Colonic diverticulosis is noted." When I asked "Big Jewels" and his assistant doctor about these terrible findings, they laughed. They said I was a healthy older man with no cancer with less than average normal bumps and bruises for my age. It seemed when the radiologists couldn't find cancer he went wild finding anything they could to write about proffering too much knowledge. Being called a degenerate with sclerotic lesions is like calling a woman of a certain age old! It hurts.

On December 17th I received the final results of a MR HEAD W/ WO CONTRAST, basically an MRI of my head. To quote radiologist Dr. Linnell's report: "No evidence of residual or recurrent lymphoma. Normal brain for age." Recall that I had these findings before making the final decision on radiation. Then on December 19th I received the final results of a CT CHEST W CONTRAST, basically a body CAT scan. To quote radiologist Dr. Green's findings: "1) No evidence of lymphoma in the chest, 2) Coronary atherosclerosis." Then Dr. Green went on to praise me with "No evidence of metastatic disease is present in the skeleton." Not leaving any stone unturned, he stated "Moderate degenerative disease is present in the midthoracic spine where there is also mild multilevel vertebral body height loss and exuberant osteophyte formation anteriorly." I could have saved him the trouble since I know I have lost some body height defying gravity for 77 years. Also hitting overheads and skiing the bumps can compact a man.

Finally, looking at the same CAT scan Dr. Keating, another radiologist, couldn't help adding to my list of woes. I quote: "Hip effusions with findings of chronic synovitis, left greater than right." His findings reminded me of a hunting dog turning up ground squirrels when I was hunting rabbits. He also identified two inconsequential small hernias. This is what I referred to earlier about knowing too much. Now if I don't hurt, which I don't, maybe I'm not the new-age sensitive guy I thought I was. I guess the important point here is that in spite of the good doctors looking into every nook and cranny of my body they found a few kitchen sinks but no cancer! Yet I was still headed for radiation. In my research I found out that all the fancy tests taken together are capable of only about 82% accuracy in predicting survival rates.

As predicted once the radiation started so did the side effects. Whenever I met folks, infrequently due to my compromised immune system, they commented on how healthy I looked, like I just returned from the Caribbean. Radiation provided me with glowing sunburn on my cracking cheeks – very healthy looking! Inside my mouth sores appeared. Nose bleeds started. A lethargy and weakness set in making it apparent that my ski racing ambitions were over for the season. It was hard to tell whether my tiredness was due to the after-effects of four months of chemo or the radiation, or both. Dr. Wallace had it about right when he said it took about one month to recover for every month in chemotherapy. Now with radiation on top of the chemo who knew?

During chemo and radiation Sigi and I would take walks on the rural roads and trails near my house, until it got too cold. January and February 2015 were the second coldest and the coldest months in Vermont recorded history going back to 1834. The average daily temperature averaged 4* for January and -2* for February. Nevertheless we tried to get as much exercise as possible during my treatments. The cold weather tended to drive folks indoors where they enjoyed each others company in confined spaces, off limits to a compromised immune systems like mine. We became trapped in my house not wanting to risk socializing with germ carriers. Reading 2-3 books a week and writing this narrative went some way to alleviate cancer inflicted boredom.

The flu was in Vermont. I mentioned to "Big Jewels" that I was about to get a flu shot. He said to go ahead, but that it wouldn't do any good due to my already compromised immune system. I saved the hole in the arm. He also said that going on our long planned trip to South America during the holiday season would be foolhardy with a nonfunctioning immune system. Sitting in an airtight aluminum tube with 200+ germ-carrying passengers for 18 hours would be asking to be infected; and then to spend three weeks in the tropics during the Southern Hemisphere summer would get me if the air travel didn't. The well planned and much anticipated three-week trip was canceled. Big Jewels wrote a letter to American Airlines (AA) stating that my medical condition prevented me from traveling. After seven emails with documentation to AA, after two letters of complaint to the Aviation Consumer Protection Division of the US Department of Transportation, and after nine months delay after the flights were canceled, I was refunded the prepaid fares of $3,833.26, according to industry standards. AA easily resold our tickets canceled three month before the actual flights, most probably at a higher fare, on the very popular usually sold-out flights. The point here is that cancer treatments compromise/upset one's lifestyle including planned travel, simple exercise, social contact, and work.

HOPE LODGE

All during my four months of chemo treatment we commuted to Burlington. This required 2-3 trips a week. From August to November the 52-mile run over hill and dale was practical, half the journey being on local roads and half on Interstate 89. When I agreed to do radiation treatments after chemo the regular daily travel to the hospital in Burlington was not possible. Vermont winter weather is simply too unpredictable to have me showing up at precisely at a prescheduled time for 17 continuous weekdays. The nursing staff at the Oncology/Radiology department recommended we check out the Hope Lodge, where I could stay during the week. Sig and I visited the Lodge. An elderly volunteer lady kindly gave us a grand tour

Hope Lodge is located 300 yards from the main entrance to UVMC. The lodge is funded to a large extent by the American Cancer Society (ACS). Having made contributions to the ACS over the years I never dreamt that I would ever be a beneficiary of an ACS program. I was satisfied that I was making a small contribution to a society dedicated to eradicating a disease that killed my mother at age 46. Now that I had become a victim of cancer myself, the offer of a place to stay close to the hospital strictly for cancer patients and their caregivers became an unexpected blessing. The Oncology/Radiation Department conveyed my radiation program to Hope Lodge. The next day a staffer from the Lodge telephoned advising us that a space in the lodge was reserved for me covering the three and a half weeks needed for my 17 radiation sessions. This period ran from December 29 to January 20.

The Lodge is a purpose-built building with 16 suites. Constructed in 2006 the new lodge replaced a large old Victorian house that previously served as the lodge for many years. Each suite includes a bedroom, a sitting room (with fold out bed), and a handicapped capable bathroom. The units can house the patient and up to two caregivers. Breakfast and dinner is served each day in a light-filled cheery dining room. Each guest unit has refrigerated and non-refrigerated space in the kitchen for food storage. This covers the guest's lunch and/or other special dietary needs. Public spaces include a dining room, a large living room, a TV room, and a conference room. There is a permanent staff of five and scores of volunteers who cook, serve meals, do maintenance, and counsel the guests. All this is available to support cancer patients and their caregivers at no expense.

The Lodge is a major locus for volunteer service. On one evening a delicious chicken potpie dinner was catered by the historic and luxurious Round Barn Inn in Waitsfield, located just four miles from my house and 50 miles away from the Lodge. I discovered in conversing with the chef and owner of the Inn that they had to wait for six months before they could get a slot to do a volunteer dinner at Hope Lodge. This competition for volunteer service covered meals: dinner, breakfast, and snacks; exhibits of art, library, and entertainment (a harpist at dinner for example). Many of the volunteers were UVMC cancer ward doctors and nurses. The immense benevolence shown cancer patients and their caregivers is truly impressive, contributing to the altruistic aura of the place.

For me this was an opportunity to interact with an amazing group of cancer patients, dedicated volunteers and angelic staff. I began to call the other guests inmates much to their amusement. The inmates came from all strata of society, mostly middle age or older, with diverse cancers. Some were rather new to cancer while others were old hands, having been under treatment for five or more years. Cancer is a great leveler. Rich, poor, young, and old barriers disappear when a common enemy rears it ugly head. Life with and after cancer can never be the same again. To be able to discuss life and cancer with so many fellow travelers was enlightening and entertaining. Below are a few examples of folks staying at Hope Lodge while I did my radiation.

One of the first fellows I met was from upper New York State. Actually about half of the inmates staying at the Lodge during my tenure were from upper New York State. Jake (52) and his fat sad eyed caregiving wife (46?) had been staying at Hope Lodge on and off for seven years. He was being treated with radiation and chemo for recurring lung cancer that had spread to his liver. A few years earlier he had his cancerous pancreas removed. This proved not to be a sufficient deterrent for him to quit smoking. When he started coughing up blood and was diagnosed with lung cancer he begrudgingly stopped smoking. Jake had seven children with his first wife and three more with his present wife, who rarely spoke due to a severe speech impediment. Another of Jake's medical conditions was epilepsy. He said he inherited it from his mother's side of the family, although he said his father's side also supplied some genetic problems he didn't explain beyond mental defects. He was saddened that many of his grown children were suffering from epilepsy, as was his first granddaughter. All of Jake's and his family's medical care was provided under Medicaid.

Other than a few odd off-the-books jobs it seems Jake never had a regular job. He was money poor and benefits rich. At the dinner table he was very entertaining. He offered unusual remedies for national and international political problems suggesting that he planned to outlive his cancer for the benefit of all society. Naturally, world leaders would be very grateful. When I asked him why he had so many children when epilepsy might be genetically transmitted to his kids he explained his strange take on Darwin's theories. Aside from the economic benefits each child's welfare payments provided he concluded that by having many children those that survived would carry his genes forward into future generations. Thinking as a taxpayer this seemed to be a very dubious and costly proposition.

Aside from all the criticisms one might make of Jake's life choices he was a courageous trooper when it came to dealing with his health issues. His cancer treatments over seven years included surgery, debilitating chemotherapy and radiation, enough to depress any human being. These ordeals and his many other medical challenges did not seem to dispirit him or dispel his natural optimism. He kindly shared his experiences of his cancer treatments with novices at the table. Each night at dinner he dug into the Lodge food with gusto, like he was on a grand cruise. Sadly, his mute wife never smiled.

I sat at dinner one evening with a man and his wife who owned a prosperous small business installing solar panels on homes. George, a big good-looking man about 50, had brain cancer. He seemed overtaken by sadness, hopelessness, chronic exhaustion, and corrosive anxiety. His very attractive wife was his business partner. Both of their sons worked in the business along with five other employees. Unlike Jake they came from families without built-in health problems, they worked very hard, and they paid taxes. At first the conversation focused on the health issues we were dealing with. With both George and me having cancer in our heads we automatically hit it off. A year earlier George had a tumor removed from inside of his scull. That tumor returned and another formed on the outside of his scull. His prospects were dim at best. His lot was last ditch surgery, chemo, and radiation. Yet he, and particularly his wife, bravely tried to be positive in a self- delusional way.

It was a time to change the subject. I asked George about the solar industry and his role in it. We had a very detailed discussion of solar technology, its future prospects for continued federal and state subsidies, and installation methodologies. Fortunately, I was able to carry on an intelligent discussion with him on the subject. As we delved into the fine points he seemed to transition from a cancer victim to a solar advocate. He persuasively convinced me that I should have fixed panels attached to my south facing standing seam roof. He assured me that he could attach solar panels without any roof penetrations by attaching the panels onto the standing seams with special brackets he invented. When we stood up after the meal his wife gave me an unexpected appreciative long hug. It was only awhile later that I realized that his wife's gratitude was due to getting George out of a dismal cancer funk, not to my bald-headed personal magnetism.

When I first saw the huge battery propelled wheel chair and the enormous 350-pound man flowing over it at the dinner table I felt a twinge of sympathy for him – obesity and cancer at the same time I thought. Herald looked to be about 40 years old. His normal sized wife, Anne, was very attentive to him. She brought dinner to him and made sure he was comfortable. Herald was affable and loquacious. He offered many theories on how to improve public education. I took a seat next to him and across from his wife. He could only fit at the end of the table. Of course the talk turned to cancer. With six people at the table, there had to be at least three cancer stories. To my amazement, Harold was just fine. It was Anne who had advanced breast cancer. The cancer had spread to her lungs and other places. It was she who was suffering from the side effects of chemo and was scheduled for surgery in a couple of weeks after chemo.

At breakfast the next morning I indelicately asked Anne how her husband became so obese. He was still sleeping. She said he was a fat but functioning elementary school teacher when he just started to balloon up to the point where he was granted a full disability by his school district. She explained that his disability included full medical insurance for life for himself and her as a dependent. They lived in upper New York State in a rural area. She explained that because of his size he couldn't drive so she drove him in their state supplied special lift-equipped van. Since he was incapable of taking care of himself she said she was his caregiver for life. Here was a case where cancer seemed to be just an additional burden to her real life burden of caring for her wheelchair bound husband. It was not my place to suggest that Harold consider a diet and getting back to work.

Earlier in my treatment while I was in a four-bay chemo station Sigi started a conversation with the wife of the man next to me that I couldn't actually see because of the intervening medical equipment. She said I should speak with him since he was a professional guitar player. After my chemo bags were empty I stopped at his chair to meet Earl. When Earl learned that I played the five-string banjo (slightly) and the guitar (less slightly) we happily carried on an animated conversation while Sigi somewhat impatiently waited to get to Costco. I didn't expect to see Earl again. In fact, of all the approximately 24 patients that I shared a chemo bay with over a four-month period Earl was the only one I saw again. Near the beginning of my Hope Lodge stay Earl showed up with two fine Martin guitars, a Stratocaster, and two fiddles.

Over the last seven years Earl was a regular at Hope Lodge. It started with pancreatic cancer, developed into colon cancer, and now afflicted his lungs. Most of the time he walked around with a fanny pack of chemo around his waist with a fine tube running up to his collar and then down to an implanted port on his chest, very much like the one I had. He was always in good humor looking for other inmates to share his inexhaustible bluegrass stories. He personally knew all the players in Bill Monroe's bluegrass band. His wife (Cora) of 50 years was his caretaker, although she herself suffered from a failed knee replacement. Consequently until Earl could get behind the wheel again his long time friend and musical partner fiddler Donnie, a superstar bluegrass musician, did the driving.

Earl owned 120 acres of land and a farmhouse in upper New York state. The land originally belonged to his grandfather. His plan was to sell the land back to his neighbor, the grandson of the person his grandfather bought the land from thereby reuniting this historic family farm. While in the Army Earl guarded the Panama Canal. After military service he had jobs in maintenance and truck driving. For hobbies he track-raced motorcycles, farmed, and attended blue grass festivals. Always at the center of his life was music, the kind you made yourself. Today he was beating down cancer with good blue grass music. It is near impossible to feel self-pity when you are singing and playing bluegrass.

Over my three and a half weeks at Hope Lodge Earl, Donnie, and I made music on several occasions much to the great pleasure of our fellow inmates. Those who couldn't stand the bluegrass music self regulated. We played after dinner in the big living room in front of the fireplace. On one occasion a friend of mine from Warren joined us with his fine guitar work. Bluegrass dispels evil thoughts and destroys cancer if only momentarily. There is no other musical form that can dispel anxiety better than bluegrass.

One evening in the lodge living room I spoke with a distinguished gentleman and his wife. He dressed for dinner in a nice coat and tie; his wife was well turned out in a stylish dress, not the usual jeans and sweatshirt common in the Lodge. After we ended our gig in the living room, basically when Earl couldn't think of any more songs, the man in his 60's said he was undergoing major abdominal cancer surgery the next afternoon for metastasized prostrate cancer. He said the optimism of the music put him in a happy place. Being aware of how sick Earl himself was and that Earl was still making glorious bluegrass music inspired him to "suck-it-up" as my sons would say. The music drove out hopelessness.

At breakfast one morning I met Jean, a second-round breast cancer victim. She was declared cured five years earlier. She wore a smart business suit that added to her aura of professionalism and tennis trim good health. A busy practicing psychiatrist from Burlington in her mid 60's her striking short cropped white hair was a marker of earlier chemo infusions. After the almost obligatory inquiries about each other's cancer she volunteered that since I lived in Warren that I might know her cousin who just built a new house on Roxbury Gap. It turns out that I not only knew her cousin, but he was quite a good friend. Indeed he came to my Super Bowl party every year and we skied together. The main point here is that cancer is ubiquitous. Even with only 16 suites one is pretty sure of meeting someone with common friends at Hope Lodge.

I was informed that Susan, a volunteer holistic healer, would be at the Lodge the next day. My back was still hurting from excessive snow shoveling thee weeks earlier. I imagined a nice massage perhaps with some hot rocks on my back couldn't be bad. The "healer" set up in the conference room on the lower floor. Curtains were pulled over the glass door and windows. She was a nice looking middle-aged woman with an engaging smile. She told me she worked with pendulums to plot the body's force lines. She was chewing gum. This reminded me of a strange admonition that my mother told me: "never trust gum-chewing professionals."

She had me mount a portable bed and elevated it to a level she could work her pendulums. She checked out my body's flow lines and did not like what she found, too many channels blocked, particularly those going to ground. This took about 30 minutes of observing the swing of the sterling silver pendulum. Foucault's swing over the force lines appeared to be the standard of reference. It was when the pendulum swung counterclockwise that the trouble became apparent. Compared to the chemo the side effects I suffered what she was doing seemed benign. She asked me to get up for more consultation.

Back on the ground she took a deck of big funny looking cards out of a nice wood box. She shuffled the cards carefully, maybe 10 times. With the skill of a riverboat poker player she fanned the cards on the table and asked me to pick one. Realizing that what I did next could mean a cancer cure or a miserable death I was careful not to take the most obvious card that seemed to stick out from the fan of cards. I picked one that was almost totally obscured going for the real truth. We read the card together in unison of horoscopic gobbledygook. The writing on the card spoke in such multi-meaning phrases that neither she nor I felt a cure was attained. The obvious conclusion was more sessions were needed to get to the bottom of my problems.

I met with Susan one more time. I would be leaving Hope Lodge the next day. We both knew this session would be our last together since her regular practice was focused on the Champlain Valley and I lived too far away in the Mad River Valley. At this session once I was flat on my back on the examination bed she used her hands to communicate with my force fields. In our previous session she may have detected a doubt in my engineering mind that a plumb-bob or pendulum could connect with my force fields - gravity yes, force fields are a stretch. I had my eyes closed and couldn't see her hand movement, but in a vague way I sensed her hands gliding over my body from head to toe. She didn't touch me but I thought I felt her. Was I becoming a believer?

Back on the ground at the table she said she detected an improvement in my force fields. She asked if I could sense an improvement. Not wanting to be an ingrate I said I was more relaxed during our second session. I didn't tell her that my back seemed to be about the same. She told me I needed to do more meditation to consolidate the work so far. She lamented that we would not be able to continue to a full balancing of my force fields. I resigned myself to let my back heal itself the natural way over time.

As I left she showed me her brochure, which she let me have. Some of the benefits of her healing included: "decreases pain such as from arthritis, facilitates wound healing, strengthens the immune system, and speeds recovery from medical treatments." On the face of it her healing was spot on for what I needed. Unfortunately, my back soreness did not yield to her approach even after two sessions with her. I didn't feel confident enough to ask her for a back rub given that my flows of energy from her perspective were the source of all my problems. As we said good-by she was still chewing gum. Perhaps I unfairly defeated her valiant attempts to help me because of my skepticism and my mother's warning.

A final few thoughts on Hope Lodge should be shared. It is important to mention that the guests could come and go as they pleased. In my case I returned home each Friday and returned each Monday. Once you were assigned a space it was yours for the duration of your treatments. You were given a key to your suite and the outside doors. No maid service was provided. There was a linen closet in each suite with extra clean sheets and towels for the guests to use as they pleased. There are 40 Hope Lodges mostly on the East Coast. Plans are in place to build many more across the country. One of the guests during my stay was a woman from Texas. Her sister was dying from brain cancer in the hospital. She told me if it were not for Hope Lodge she could not afford to be by her sister's side over the time it is taking her to die.

The American Cancer Society (ASC) and other cancer research organizations mostly raise funds by appealing to those who are looking to find a cure to this terrible disease. It is very special that the ACS is supporting the Hope Lodge network and recognizing the need to support those afflicted right now – those living with the cancer experience. This is not to say that research is unimportant. However, spending some precious resources on the care of those enduring the disease with lodging when desperately needed is right on!

MEDICAL COSTS

So far nowhere has the cost of cancer treatment been mentioned. Being 77 years old means I have Medicare. I do not have any other medical insurance other than basic Medicare. Supplemental insurance and HMO coverage are quite popular among Medicare recipients. My analysis taken from the perspective of exceptional good health convinced me to stay with basic Medicare only. I could have paid additional annual premiums to cover all my cancer costs. These premiums over my 12 years of Medicare would have exceeded my out of pocket cancer costs. Insurance companies make money by charging premiums that will cover their medical liabilities, operating expenses, and profits. An interesting aside, since Obama Care was enacted medical insurance companies stock prices have increased 30%. I am not recommending my insurance decisions to anyone. Each person must decide how to handle his or her own medical expenses based on their individual economic and health circumstances.

At no time during my treatment did I feel pressured for how I was going to pay for all my medical costs. Up front I made it clear to the UVMC that my only insurance coverage was basic federal Medicare. Each time I checked in for a service my coverage was confirmed. This in some way seemed to simplify the payment system. I am sure that UVMC checked out my credit rating and perhaps other sources to check whether I would be good for the expenses. Medicare pays for about 80% of medical costs. However the system is so complex it defies understanding. In my case Medicare paid for 80% of my cancer costs. I paid the balance out of my savings. UVMC sent me bills monthly, sometimes more than one. I did review them making sure that I received the services billed to the extent I understood the technical jargon on the bills. Basically, I paid the bills as they came in.

Each quarter Medicare sends me a summary of my account status. I have been receiving these statements for 12 years and can honestly say that they are indecipherable. Charges seem to be subtly adjusted by Medicare and the vendors. If codified this "system" would be a harder code to break than the famous Enigma machine the Germans used during WW II. I get the impression that hospitals can charge according to the depth and type of the pocket of the payee. One thing I do know is exactly how much I paid out of pocket for my cancer treatment. After adding up all the costs this is an approximate summary:

1)	UVMC	$19,000
2)	Dana-Farber	200
3)	Central Vermont Medical Center	150
4)	Mad River Health Center	200
5)	Misc. Prescriptions	250
6)	Travel	1,500
	Total	21,300

While at Hope Lodge over half of the folks I met seemed to be on Medicaid, a federal program that essentially pays for all medical costs, no co-pays or deductibles. In conversations about medical costs at Hope Lodge many folks were amazed that I was actually paying for cancer treatments that they had been receiving for many years totally free, including all their other medical expenses. One woman suggested that I must be one of the 1%ers. In reality my income, including my mandatory distribution from my IRA, my Social Security, and investment income amounts to about the average household income in Vermont. Over 35% of Vermonters have totally subsidized health care. With Medicare, while I'm not totally covered, I feel well treated by the federal government and my fellow taxpayers. Paying anything around $20,000 for an illness that cost well over $100,000 is clearly a bargain

In all my contact with the UVMC I detected no differences in the way services were delivered to patients; that is to say both the rich and the poor received the same medical procedures based on their health needs rather than their ability to pay. Indeed those on Medicaid might even be better off than tax paying middle class folks who may be more restrained in seeking medical services that they will have to pay for out of pocket, at least partially.

Back when raising my middle-class family in Washington, DC I was envious of friends who were able to get Medicaid or had fat medical coverage by their employers. They rushed to the doctor or hospital for even minor medical issues like a cold while I told my kids to tough it out at home with an aspirin. As I remember it, my employer policy had a deductible of $600. In the 1970's this was considered generous. About every other year my family used up the deductible and were fully covered after a co pay of 10% for additional medical expenses like appendectomies for my two sons and female maladies for my wife. In those days before the widespread utilization of Medicaid there was an obvious discrepancy between the economic classes. The poor excessively used "free" emergency rooms at hospitals while getting very little preventative care. This gap is closing. Today most of the poor seem to do quite well in the medical system with Medicaid and other subsidies. This is reflected in the income-blind uniform standard of care provided at places like UVMC.

SURVIVAL

One never really "survives" cancer. That is cancer is never over and done. In the course of my disease I have discussed survival with scores of cancer "survivors." They all admitted that yes, they survived for now, but they will never be without the doubt that cancer could return in one of its many forms. Ignorance is a form bliss one might say. Having cancer shatters that bliss forever. This does not mean all hope is lost. Quite the contrary, the experience of cancer sharpens the appetite for life. Lance Armstrong admits that he would never have become one of the world's great athletes unless he had the dreaded disease. Through his foundation, now called Livestrong, he has raised over $500 million for cancer research. Thankfully, being one of the world's biggest liars and most successful dopers in a sport renowned for dopers for so long probably had nothing to do with his cancer. Nevertheless, the appreciation of the importance of each day hits us on the head after a personal encounter with cancer. It also makes us examine our lives with a better perspective of the meaning of mortality.

A good example of this in literature is a book by Randy Pausch and Jeffery Zaslow, "The Last Lecture." It is the story of a professor with terminal pancreatic cancer conveying everything he wanted his children to know after his death, in essence the meaning of life. The book was on the "New York Times" best-seller list for 112 weeks starting in 2008 lasting until 2011.

The experience of cancer is very personal. Each of us has our individual take on the ordeal. No matter what help we get from the medical community it is still our very own disease. The patient and their caregiver are the center. The cancer patient is responsible and ultimately in charge of coordinating their treatment, up to their individual capability. This is necessary due to the incredible specialization of the practice of medicine, illustrated by the number of doctors involved in my singular case. None of whom coordinated all the details of my diagnosis and treatment.

During the diagnosis phase I saw five doctors not including the services of two radiologists and a pathologist, that is 8 doctors before I had the final diagnosis and a single bit of treatment. The first three doctors after going down dead ends finally discovered I had a tumor in my head. Then it was off to see the Eyes, Ears, Nose and Throat specialists at UVMC. These two doctors along with a pathologist were able to make the final diagnosis: aggressive non-Hodgkin's lymphoma in my sinus area. I am in awe of the high quality of medical care I received during this period. Before cancer is a certainty in an otherwise healthy person more likely possibilities explaining the symptoms needed to be explored.

The treatment phase included 11 more doctors. They include two oncologists, a radiation/oncologist, a surgical doctor, a pharmacist, two pathologists, an emergency room doctor, and three radiologists. Included here are the two doctors at Dana-Farber offering the second opinion and consultation. Not included are the many nurse practitioners, nurses, and support personnel at UVMC numbering up to 50 different individuals or more. Not to get into too much detail these good doctors got me through chemotherapy, the surgical implantation of my chest port, radiation therapy, and extensive testing. At first my number one oncologist, Dr. "Big Jewels" Sprague, was coordinating all my treatments. This seemed to break down due to interdepartmental communications within UVMC discussed earlier and moving on to the Oncology/Radiation Department. It is perhaps amazing that with all these highly trained people dealing with a complicated disease coordination is possible at all. It is a long time ago when one went to the doctor and perhaps with one specialist got treated for a serious illness. In sum my treatment required the services of 19 doctors.

UVMC cancer doctors do meet regularly to discuss cancer cases hospital wide. This is essential to get the best ideas of the doctors for treatment and to coordinate individual patient treatment. I know my case was discussed more than once. In addition whenever a service was provided by the hospital a "visit summary" was provided to each patient covering both procedures and medications. The hospital was very meticulous in identifying and re-identifying patients at each visit. This only failed one time in my case when I was called for a service. When the nurse discovered that I grew four inches and gained 50 pounds she began to suspect I must be the wrong Michael out of the gang in the waiting room. Today the family doctor is the gateway to the larger extremely complex specialized medical treatment community. Once in that community the patient needs to take control, at a minimum to make an effort to understand their treatment and to help coordinate what is being done to them.

As discussed earlier there is nothing more profound than confronting one's mortality. One morning in the waiting room before a chemo treatment I was sitting next to a man and his wife. He was bald like me. With a common disease there is instant empathy for the poor soul next to you. He told me that having cancer was the best thing that had happened to him in the 56 years of his life. His wife nodded in agreement. He said since being diagnosed with a life threatening cancer he turned his life around. Cancer was the reason he was "born again" in Christ. Before his affliction he said his life was drifting without meaning in both his personal relations and his business dealings. Now he had purpose and a clear vision of his place in the grand scheme of things. One had to admire his faith. In a slight way I envied him. Like Saint Paul he was blinded then saved by a resurrected Jesus, not on the road to Damascus but rather on the way to chemotherapy. I wished him well when I was called to begin my infusion.

Years ago during my days in Washington DC I worked closely with the President of the American Institute of Architects, Archibald Rogers. He had narrowly escaped death by decapitation when a huge piece of plaster from the ceiling of his pre- revolutionary historic home in Annapolis fell onto his bed just where his head would have been a few minutes earlier. The plaster broke the bed in two. He calmly told me this story the very day of the accident while we dined at the Institute. When I expressed wonderment over his matter of fact recounting of the event he said life was all about dying well. That he was at the pinnacle of his career and didn't worry about just having missed being killed surprised me. He explained that dying well had nothing to do with a shorter or longer existence on the planet, but rather a continuing satisfaction with life as it was lead. Not a religious man he nevertheless was ready to meet his maker any time it happened. It took cancer for me to understand what he was saying.

When I was in high school receiving religious instruction the priests would attempt to hone our sense of guilt and then offer redemption through the sacraments of the Catholic Church. My meager sense of guilt was inversely proportional to my sense of immortality. This was problematic throughout my life until cancer. I am bit like the waiting room "born again" man and Arch Rogers combined. An examined readiness for mortality waited until cancer then it was discovered to be there all along.

Woody Allen once said he was not afraid of death, he just didn't want to there when it happened. With modern medicine concentrated on the front end of life with little effort on the end of life he was unfortunately right on. Death is so very much part of the human experience the mechanics of it are curiously under developed. A fellow sailor from my sailing club has been very active in the "Death With Dignity" legislation in Vermont. The law basically excuses doctors and hospitals from law suits should someone decide that terminal illness makes life unlivable and litigious relatives have second thoughts. Preserving an untenable life at all costs to the patient is both cruel and unnecessary. On the other hand the modern Hospice Movement is a blessing to cancer patients being cured and not being cured as it can provide the prospect of a more gentle ending than one of just more pain and suffering. Woody, the fact is we are all going to be there when death happens. Lets be more humane.

Finally, my cancer, win, lose, or draw (can there be a draw with cancer?) informed my life in two ways. First of all it propelled me into acknowledging that I was indeed an old man, not a young person in an old body. The reality of being in the last ten years of one's life is like graduating from university prepared to start a major new chapter in one's life. Perhaps my sister Lori put it succinctly by asking rhetorically: "Haven't you won enough skiing races?" Secondly, this is not a singular journey. The love and support from hundreds of family, friends, and acquaintances reminded me that you don't get sick and die alone. This I knew already when family and close friends passed.

They all took some of me with them and left some of themselves with me. Cancer struck this reality home like the great golden spike.

Today there is no evidence of lymphoma in my body, as near as it is possible to determine. There will be tests over the next five years to see if a technical cure has been affected. However, in my case after my 4-month check up, while no cancer was found, it was determined that I had contracted myelodysplasia (MDS) due to the chemotherapy drugs. This is a disease of the bone marrow that impairs the body's ability to produce both red and white cells. This condition can occur quite quickly after chemo, my case, and also can occur many years after chemo or not at all. After more blood work and a new bone and marrow sample "Big Jewels" recommended I seek treatment for this condition at Dana-Farber in Boston where a special department deals specifically with this malady. The symptom of myelodysplasia is constant fatigue. I expect that this, one might say, is an extension of my cancer treatment, an example of never really escaping the realities of cancer.

The Rest of the Story

Unfortunately my cancer story does not end with a successful cure of my lymphoma. As discussed earlier bad cells are indigenous to all of us. The body's ability to destroy bad cells can be compromised in many ways: by being exposed to carcinogens such as tobacco smoke, ionizing radiation, organic chemicals, heavy metals, herbicides, pesticides, fertilizers, and petroleum derivatives. The very chemicals that were used to kill off my lymphoma tumor also attacked my bone marrow cells. This is called myelodysplastic syndrome, MDS. MDS affects about 10,000 people a year. About one in six of those who have had Rchop chemotherapy get MDS. It occurs predominantly in older patients. It can occur quite quickly after chemotherapy or many years later, possibly even occurring five years or more after chemo. One could say I got unlucky. I was one out of six.

How did my new cancer develop? My lymphoma chemotherapy was completed on November 21st, 2014. My radiation therapy was completed on January 20, 2015. The next date with my cancer doctors was scheduled for May 11th, 2015 for a follow up checkup four months after I was, at least on paper, cured. On December 9th, 2014 I had a complete body CAT scan showing no cancer. On January 9th, 2015 I had an enhanced MRI of my head showing no tumor. Blood analysis also showed no cancer cells present. Clinically I was cured of lymphoma! Happy day!

On March 24th, 2015 I went to my general doctor, Fran Cook, for an annual wellness exam covered, and encouraged by, Medicare. I complained to him that I was still not feeling up to my old self. He did an exam and concluded I was in good health and attributed my malaise to the lingering effects of chemo and radiation. My blood showed that I was not anemic – hemoglobin came in at 13.2 well above the 11.3 reading at the end of chemo suggesting that my blood was springing back after being compromised during chemo.

Normal range for hemoglobin is 12.3 to 18.3. When I started chemo my hemoglobin was a healthy 13.9. At the beginning I did regular exercises each day. By the end of chemo I could barely do 50% of my formerly regular exercises. The hemoglobin that carries oxygen to the muscles was reduced by 30% then sprang back to normal range when measured at the wellness exam. Good news!

Another important blood factor that controls the immune system typically compromised during chemo treatments is white blood cell count (WBC). It too improved after chemo ended. Good news!

This gave me the confidence to get on a germ-filled airplane and travel to Thousand Oaks in California to spend Easter with my son Matt and his family. Remember that Sigi and I had to cancel our planned lifetime trip to South America over the 2014/2015 Christmas Holidays on doctor's orders due to my compromised immune system during chemo treatment. When the immune system is down one is very likely to catch all kinds of diseases, such as simple colds and much worse. One of the biggest compromises in lifestyle during chemo is staying relatively isolated to hide from potential infection. With a clean bill of health from Dr. Cook I was looking forward to getting back to our modest social scene in the Mad River Valley and beyond.

The shock came during my four-month follow up visit with my oncologist, "Big Jewels" Sprague on May 12th, 2015. My blood work showed that my blood was turning into water. It was so bad that Dr. Sprague asked me to come in the next day to take a bone and marrow sample that he would do himself. The pathology reports on my bone and marrow showed that I had contracted MDS as a result of the chemotherapy to rid myself of lymphoma. "Big Jewels" seemed to be upset by this development. He advised me that UVMC did not have all the medical technology needed to deal with this deadly disease. He recommended that I seek help from Dana-Farber, and specifically Dr. David Steensma, Chair of the bone cancer department.

On June 9th, 2015 my friend Gunner drove Sigi and me to Dana-Farber hospital in Boston. Gunnar crews on my race boat. He is a retired immigration attorney who lives in Shelburne Vermont and used to practice in Boston. His offer to drive was kindly and we didn't want to get lost. Gunnar also needed to replenish his wine and spirits cellar at the gigantic New Hampshire State discount liquor store on Route 89 on the way to Boston. Both chores were accomplished with alacrity.

They took six tubes of blood before I even saw a doctor at Dana/ Farber. Eventually, Three doctors who specialize in bone cancer examined me. Dr. Steensma proposed I begin chemotherapy using azacitidine (commercially known as Vidaza). The purpose of the drug is to shock the bone marrow to start producing cells again, primarily by killing off the bad blast cells that had been displacing my bone marrow cells. In the process as chemo does, it also kills off some good cells. I agreed and it was determined that I could take the injections at UVMC in Vermont. The process is a 28-day cycle up to six times, two injections in the stomach fat seven consecutive days then a 21-day reprieve. I completed five cycles with no evidence of improvement. The Friday before the beginning of the sixth cycle my temperature was 102*. I was simply too sick to endure another Vidaza cycle.

Usually, by the fourth cycle some improvement should be detected. In my case there was none. Therefore I stopped Vidaza.

To stay alive while doing the Vidaza I needed a two-pint transfusion of type O (negative) blood about every two weeks. My critical blood counts are a disaster. For example my white blood cell count is 0.6 (normal is 3.5-10.5). This means once again I have virtually no immune system. My hemoglobin hovers around 8 (normal 12.3-18.3). Trying to lead a reasonable lifestyle while undergoing these treatments is impossible. However I was able occasionally race my boat on Lake Champlain with a strong young crew. Otherwise I remained around the house. A beautiful house in a pristine environment is some consolation. Many days just climbing one flight of stairs had me gasping for breath. All this is not me! Being cheerful in cancer treatment for over a year with slim prospects of a cure takes a lot of character, but it is not unlimited. The cure rate for MDS is 2%, that is survival for 5 years.

During the five months I was being treated with Vidaza I had many of the side effects associated with the drug. When asked how I was feeling I responded, not very well. This feeling of un-wellness can be broken down into its component parts to get a better picture. I share this not to curry sympathy or to belabor the point that cancer is hell, rather only to let the reader how it is.

Weakness, slight nausea, light headache, dizziness, fatigue, and apathy all gang up. It's remarkable that I was able to sit here at my kitchen table to write this. The weakness comes from cells being killed by the Vidaza, both good and bad. The headache and dizziness comes from compromised blood - not enough oxygen getting to the brain and muscle tissue. This is augmented by chemically induced cardiac rhythm disturbances (atrial fibrillation) weakening the pumping function of the heart, also caused by Vidaza and lack of white blood cells. The fatigue and apathy is the body screaming out for relief from the chemical poisons being injected to "cure" MDS. As I constantly point out to Big Jewels and any other medical worker available I was a perfectly healthy person until I started being "cured" from various cancers. How to turn a perfectly healthy athletic body into a pathetic wreck? Start with cancer.

The course ahead was strewn with shoals. Dr. Sprague asked for another bone and marrow sample as he suspected the bad cell blasts in my bone marrow had progressed to leukemia. On November 17 Dr. Sprague did the required procedure to obtain the samples from both of my hips. The results proved that Dr. Sprague was right in his suspicions. My MDS had turned into full-blown case of leukemia. More bad luck!

Dr. Sprague and I consulted with Dr. Steensma at Dana-Farber to consider future treatments. For treating the MDS and /or leukemia it seemed that a drug called REVLIMID held some promise. However, if it affected me the some way as Vidaza it would be a very tough, months long, life-compromising endurance experiment with the high probability of little or no benefit. A global search ensued for clinical trials for attacking my disease with "targeted therapy" involving my own stem cells. They existed but had little success to date. This goes back to my earlier observation that my cancer came five years too soon to get any help from these new approaches. In our research we found two clinical trails in China, two at the medical school at the University of Pennsylvania, and one at Dana-Farber in Boston. Dr. Steensma also knew of several others in the US. None fit my exact case. It would be a long shot for any benefit.

These new therapies involve removing the patient's blood, extracting the stem cells (or others) in a hospital stay of about a week. Then the cells, after being modified to be cancer-killing cells, are re injected into the patient to attack the specific cancer. The procedures related to this kind of therapy are difficult on the patient. Unfortunately, none of the clinical trials attacked my exact cell structure, and very few were successful. In order for me to enter a clinical trail I would have to be continuously treated for my disease and on top of that endure the debilitation of the trial itself. After being so sick during the Vidaza treatment I felt that to do both another chemotherapy and a clinical trail at the same time would be untenable.

This is now getting very serious. All the earlier talk of dealing with mortality is now front and center. I asked both Dr. Sprague and Dr. Steensma what they would do if they had my disease. Both of then said they would go into home Hospice care. Their assessment is that doing another chemotherapy plus a clinical trail would be unproductive. It should be remembered that during my five months on Vidaza my heart was damaged causing atrial fibrillation (potential blood clots, raising my heart beat from 60 to 120 just walking to the bathroom, and extreme breathlessness), my renal function was compromised, I needed 12 transfusions, and my body generally suffered significant decline. People still said I looked good!

On December 1, 2015 I decided to take my doctor's recommendation. A visiting nurse visited on that very day. She stopped by my house in the afternoon to sign me up with the Central Vermont Home & Hospice. Nurse Joanne is Japanese, 60 years old. She practiced in San Francisco for number of years before settling in Vermont. On Friday December 4th I had my last transfusion. Transfusions are not given after the Hospice program starts; this would be considered palliative care. This is the big decision because I could have stayed alive for a few more months by taking regular transfusions. Given the quality of life I decided it was not worth suffering more months for the same inevitable conclusion.

When you read this I will be at peace having had a full 77 years of exceptional life well lived. I must admit that the 18 months of being "cured" of cancer was on the miserable side. All the Kings horses and all the Kings men (that is modern medicine) couldn't put me back together again. I believe I received the best medicine available. Generally I would say that all of my doctors, nurses, and support staff were exceptionally dedicated and skilled.

I am confident that in five years the particular kinds of cancer that afflicted me will be much more curable and treatable. Specifically, treatment will be aimed at cancer cells only, sparing healthy cells, thereby greatly reducing the bad side effects of the old style chemotherapy- in my case leading to MDS and leukemia.

So now I bid you all goodbye, good health, and good luck in the years ahead. You will have the benefit of better medicine, better health, and a better life with bacon, cheese, butter, and cream.

About the Author

Michael Barker earned degrees in engineering, architecture, and city and regional planning from the University of California, Berkeley. He worked in the planning field in California, the United Kingdom, Vermont, and Washington, DC. Barker lived in Vermont until his death.

Printed in the United States
By Bookmasters